This book should be returned to any branch of the
Lancashire County Library on or before the date shown

Look and Find
On the
Farm

Illustrated by
Gareth Lucas

Designed by Ruth Russell
Written by Kirsteen Robson

The answers
are on pages
30–32.

4

5

9

16

19

Which duck is diving for food?

Find three fish that are exactly the same.

How many frogs can you spy?

20

Spot two boats.

Where has the farmer left his paintbrush?

21

23

29

ANSWERS

There are 10 tractors: 4 are on page 1, there's 1 on page 12 and 5 more on page 28.

1

There are 6 milk churns.

2-3

4-5

6-7

There are 9 spiders.

8-9

10–11

12–13

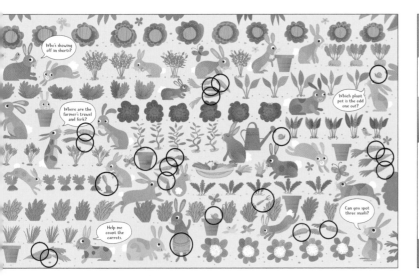

There are 15 carrots.

There are 7 ladders.

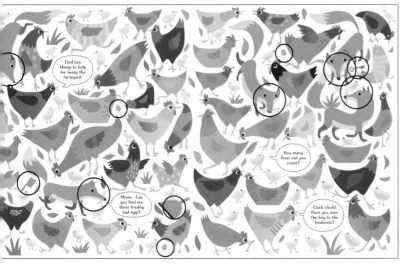

There are 5 foxes.

There are 6 frogs.

ANSWERS (continued)

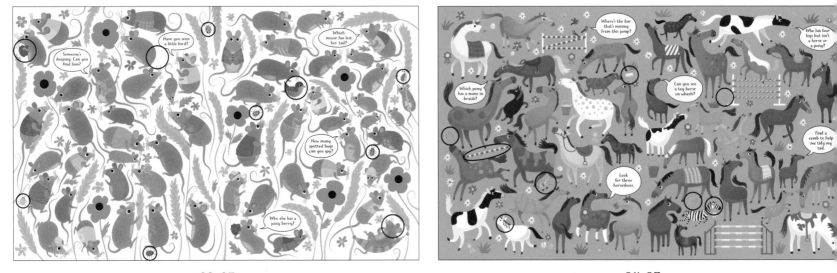

There are 6 spotted bugs. 22-23

24-25

There are 4 mice. 26-27

28-29 There are 5 more field m